Preparation for TAKS

Practice Tests
for Grade 11: Exit Level English Language Arts

Two Practice Tests:
- **Reading Selections, Visual Representations, and Items**
- **Writing Prompts**
- **Revising and Editing Passages and Items**

HOLT, RINEHART AND WINSTON

A Harcourt Education Company

Austin • Orlando • Chicago • New York • Toronto • London • San Diego

TABLE OF CONTENTS

Practice Test 1

Practice Test 2

TAKS Test Information

Grade 11
TAKS Practice Test 1

- **Reading Selections, Visual Representation, and Items**
- **Writing Prompt**
- **Revising and Editing Passage 1 and Items**
- **Revising and Editing Passage 2 and Items**

DIRECTIONS

Read these selections and the visual representation. When you are finished, answer the questions that follow.

As this part of the story begins, John and Gertrude Delahanty are awaiting the arrival of Mr. and Mrs. Kibbler and their son Edwin. Mrs. Kibbler has asked to meet with the Delahantys because she believes that their daughter Cress was responsible for Edwin losing some of his teeth.

Then He Goes Free

by Jessamyn West

Reading notes

1 Mr. Delahanty went to the door while Mrs. Delahanty stood in the back of the room by the fireplace unwilling to take one step toward meeting her visitors.

2 Mrs. Kibbler was a small woman with a large, determined nose, prominent blue eyes and almost no chin. Her naturally curly hair—she didn't wear a hat—sprang away from her head in a great cage-shaped pompadour[1] which dwarfed her face.

3 Behind Mrs. Kibbler was Mr. Kibbler, short, dusty, soft-looking, bald, except for a fringe of hair about his ears so thick that the top of his head, by contrast, seemed more naked than mere lack of hair could make it.

4 Behind Mr. Kibbler was Edwin Jr. He was as thin as his mother, as mild and soft-looking as his father; and to these qualities he added an unhappiness all of his own. He gave one quick look at the room and the Delahantys through his thick-lensed spectacles, after which he kept his eyes on the floor.

5 Mr. Delahanty closed the door behind the callers, then introduced his wife to Mrs. Kibbler. Mrs. Kibbler in turn introduced her family to the Delahantys. While the Kibblers were seating themselves—Mrs. Kibbler and Edwin Jr. on the sofa, Mr. Kibbler on a straight-backed chair in the room's darkest corner—Mrs. Delahanty, out of nervousness, bent and lit the fire, which was laid in the fireplace, though the evening was not cold enough for it. Then she and Mr. Delahanty seated themselves in the chairs on each side of the fireplace.

6 Mrs. Kibbler looked at the fire with some surprise. "Do you find it cold this evening, Mrs. Delahanty?" she asked.

1. pompadour: hairstyle in which the hair is combed up and back from the forehead.

From "Twelve Winter" (Then He Goes Free) from *Cress Delahanty* by Jessamyn West. Copyright 1948 and renewed © 1976 by Jessamyn West. Reprinted by permission of **Harcourt, Inc.** Electronic format by permission of **Russell & Volkening, Inc.**

7   "No," said Mrs. Delahanty, "I don't. I don't know why I lit the fire."

8   To this Mrs. Kibbler made no reply. Instead, without preliminaries, she turned to her son. "Edwin," she said, "show the Delahantys what their daughter did to your teeth."

9   Mrs. Delahanty wanted to close her eyes, look into the fire, or find, as Edwin Jr. had done, a spot of her own on the floor to examine. There was an almost imperceptible ripple along the length of the boy's face as if he had tried to open his mouth but found he lacked the strength. He momentarily lifted his eyes from the floor to dart a glance into the dark corner where his father sat. But Mr. Kibbler continued to sit in expressionless silence.

10   "Edwin," said Mrs. Kibbler, "speak to your son."

11   "Do what your mother says, son," said Mr. Kibbler.

12   Very slowly, as if it hurt him, Edwin opened his mouth.

13   His teeth were white, and in his thin face they seemed very large, as well. The two middle teeth, above, had been broken across in a slanting line. The lower incisor appeared to be missing entirely.

14   "Wider, Edwin," Mrs. Kibbler urged. "I want the Delahantys to see exactly what their daughter is responsible for."

15   But before Edwin could make any further effort Mrs. Delahanty cried, "No, that's enough."

16   "I didn't want you to take our word for anything," Mrs. Kibbler said reasonably. "I wanted you to see."

17   "Oh, we see, all right," said Mrs. Delahanty earnestly.

18   Mr. Delahanty leaned forward and spoke to Mrs. Kibbler. "While we see the teeth, Mrs. Kibbler, it just isn't a thing we think Crescent would do. Or in fact how she *could* do it. We think Edwin must be mistaken."

19   "You mean lying?" asked Mrs. Kibbler flatly.

20   "Mistaken," repeated Mr. Delahanty.

21   "Tell them, Edwin," said Mrs. Kibbler.

22   "She knocked me down," said Edwin, very low.

23   Mrs. Delahanty, although she was already uncomfortably warm, held her hands nearer the fire, even rubbed them together a time or two.

24   "I simply can't believe that," she said.

25   "You mean hit you with her fist and knocked you down?" asked Mr. Delahanty.

26   "No," said Edwin even lower than before. "Ran into me."

27   "But not on purpose," said Mrs. Delahanty.

28   Edwin nodded. "Yes," he said. "On purpose."

29   "But why?" asked Mr. Delahanty. "Why? Cress wouldn't do such a thing, I know—without some cause. Why?"

30   "Tell them why, Edwin," said his mother.

31   Edwin's head went even nearer the floor—as if the spot he was watching had diminished or retreated.

32   "For fun," he said.

33   It was impossible not to believe the boy as he sat there hunched, head bent, one eyelid visibly twitching. "But Cress would never do such a thing," said Mrs. Delahanty.

34   Mrs. Kibbler disregarded this. "It would not have been so bad, Mr. Delahanty, except that Edwin was standing by one of those ollas. When your daughter shoved Edwin over she shoved the <u>olla</u> over, too. That's probably what broke his teeth. Heavy as cement and falling down on top of him and breaking up in a thousand pieces. To say nothing of his being doused with water on a cold day. And Providence[2] alone can explain why his glasses weren't broken."

35   "What had you done, Edwin?" asked Mrs. Delahanty again.

36   "Nothing," whispered Edwin.

37   "All we want," said Mrs. Kibbler, "is what's perfectly fair. Pay the dentist's bill. And have that girl of yours apologize to Edwin."

38   Mrs. Delahanty got up suddenly and walked over to Edwin. She put one hand on his thin shoulder and felt him twitch under her touch like a frightened colt.

39   "Go on, Edwin," she said. "Tell me the truth. Tell me why."

40   Edwin slowly lifted his head. "Go on, Edwin," Mrs. Delahanty encouraged him.

41   "He told you once," said Mrs. Kibbler. "Fun. That girl of yours is a big, boisterous thing from all I hear. She owes my boy an apology.

42   Edwin's face continued to lift until he was looking directly at Mrs. Delahanty.

43   He started to speak—but had said only three words, "Nobody ever wants," when Cress walked in from the hall. She had evidently been there for some time, for she went directly to Edwin.

44   "I apologize for hurting you, Edwin," she said.

45   Then she turned to Mrs. Kibbler. "I've got twelve seventy-

2. Providence: the care and help of a supernatural being or force.

five saved for a bicycle. That can go to help pay for his teeth.”

46   After the Kibblers left, the three Delahantys sat for some time without saying a word. The fire had about died down and outside an owl, hunting finished, flew back toward the hills, softly hooting.

47   “I guess if we hurried we could just about catch the second show,” Mr. Delahanty said.

48   “I won't be going to shows for a while,” said Cress.

49   The room was very quiet. Mrs. Delahanty traced the outline of one of the bricks in the fireplace.

50   “I can save twenty-five cents a week that way. Toward his teeth,” she explained.

51   Mrs. Delahanty took the poker and stirred the coals so that for a second there was an upward drift of sparks; but the fire was too far gone to blaze. Because it had not yet been completely dark when the Kibblers came, only one lamp had been turned on. Now that night had arrived the room was only partially lighted; but no one seemed to care. Mr. Delahanty, in Mr. Kibbler's dark corner, was almost invisible. Mrs. Delahanty stood by the fireplace. Cress sat where Edwin had sat, looking downward, perhaps at the same spot at which he had looked.

52   “One day at school,” she said, “Edwin went out in the fields at noon and gathered wild flower bouquets for everyone. A lupine, a poppy, two barley heads, four yellow violets. He tied them together with blades of grass. They were sweet little bouquets. He went without his lunch to get them fixed, and when we came back from eating there was a bouquet on every desk in the study hall. It looked like a flower field when we came in and Edwin did it to surprise us.”

53   After a while Mr. Delahanty asked, “Did the kids like that?”

54   “Yes, they liked it. They tore their bouquets apart,” said Cress, “and used the barley beards to tickle each other. Miss Ingols made Edwin gather up every single flower and throw it in the wastepaper basket.”

55   After a while Cress said, “Edwin has a collection of bird feathers. The biggest is from a buzzard, the littlest from a hummingbird. They're all different colors. The brightest is from a woodpecker.”

56   “Does he kill birds,” Mr. Delahanty asked, “just to get a feather?”

57   “Oh, no!” said Cress. “He just keeps his eyes open to where a bird might drop a feather. It would spoil his collection to get a feather he didn't find that way.”

58   Mr. Delahanty sighed and stirred in his wooden chair so that

59   "Edwin would like to be a missionary to China," said Cress. Some particle in the fireplace as yet unburned, blazed up in a sudden spurt of blue flame. "Not a preaching missionary," she explained.

60   "A medical missionary?" asked Mr. Delahanty.

61   "Oh, no! Edwin says he's had to take too much medicine to ever be willing to make other people take it."

62   There was another long silence in the room. Mrs. Delahanty sat down in the chair her husband had vacated and once more held a hand toward the fire. There was just enough life left in the coals to make the tips of her fingers rosy. She didn't turn toward Cress at all or ask a single question. Back in the dusk Cress's voice went on.

63   "He would like to teach them how to play baseball."

64   Mr. Delahanty's voice was matter-of-fact. "Edwin doesn't look to me like he would be much of a baseball player."

65   "Oh he isn't," Cress agreed. "He isn't even any of a baseball player. But he could be a baseball authority. Know everything and teach by diagram. That's what he'd have to do. And learn from them how they paint. He says some of their pictures look like they had been painted with one kind of bird feather and some with another. He knows they don't really paint with bird feathers," she explained. "That's just a fancy of his."

66   The night wind moving in off the Pacific began to stir the eucalyptus trees in the windbreak. Whether the wind blew off sea or desert, didn't matter, the long eucalyptus leaves always lifted and fell with the same watery, surflike sound.

67   "I'm sorry Edwin happened to be standing by that olla," said Mr. Delahanty. "That's what did the damage, I suppose."

68   "Oh, he had to stand there," said Cress. "He didn't have any choice. That's the mush pot."

69   "Mush pot," repeated Mr. Delahanty.

70   "It's a circle round the box the olla stands on," said Crescent. "Edwin spends about his whole time there. While we're waiting for the bus anyway."

71   "Crescent," asked Mr. Delahanty, "what is this mush pot?"

72   "It's prison," said Cress, surprise in her voice. "It's where the prisoners are kept. Only at school we always call it the mush pot."

73   "Is this a game?" asked Mr. Delahanty.

74   "It's dare base," said Crescent. "Didn't you ever play it? You choose up sides. You draw two lines and one side stands in the middle and tries to catch the other side as they run by. Nobody

ever chooses Edwin. The last captain to choose just gets him. Because he can't help himself. They call him the handicap. He gets caught first thing and spends the whole game in the mush pot because nobody will waste any time trying to rescue him. He'd just get caught again, they say, and the whole game would be nothing but rescue Edwin."

75   "How do you rescue anyone, Cress?" asked her father.

76   "Run from home base to the mush pot without being caught. Then take the prisoner's hand. Then he goes free."

77   "Were you trying to rescue Edwin, Cress?"

78   Cress didn't answer her father at once. Finally she said, "It was my duty. I chose him for our side. I chose him first of all and didn't wait just to get him. So it was my duty to rescue him. Only I ran too hard and couldn't stop. And the olla fell down on top of him and knocked his teeth out. And humiliated him. But he was free," she said. "I got there without being caught."

79   Mrs. Delahanty spoke with a great surge of warmth and anger. "Humiliated him! When you were only trying to help him. Trying to rescue him. And you were black and blue for days yourself! What gratitude."

80   Cress said, "But he didn't want to be rescued, Mother. Not by me anyway. He said he liked being in the mush pot. He said . . . he got there on purpose . . . to observe. He gave me back the feathers I'd found for him. One was a road-runner feather. The only one he had."

81   "Well, you can start a feather collection of your own," said Mr. Delahanty with energy. "I often see feathers when I'm walking through the orchard. After this I'll save them for you."

82   "I'm not interested in feathers," said Cress. Then she added, "I can get two bits an hour any time suckering[3] trees for Mr. Hudson or cleaning blackboards at school. That would be two fifty a week at least. Plus the twelve seventy-five. How much do you suppose his teeth will be?"

83   "Cress," said her father, "you surely aren't going to let the Kibblers go on thinking you knocked their son down on purpose, are you? Do you want Edwin to think that?"

84   "Edwin doesn't really think that," Cress said. "He knows I was rescuing him. But now I've apologized—and if we pay for the new teeth and everything, maybe after a while he'll believe it."

85   She stood up and walked to the hall doorway. "I'm awfully tired," she said. "I guess I'll go to bed."

86   "But Cress," asked Mrs. Delahanty, "why do you want him to believe it? When it isn't true?"

---

3. suckering: removing shoots, pruning.

87   Cress was already through the door, but she turned back to explain. "You don't knock people down you are sorry for," she said.

88   After Cress had gone upstairs Mrs. Delahanty said, "Well, John, you were right, of course."

89   "Right?" asked Mr. Delahanty, again forgetful.

90   "About Cress's being interested in the boys."

91   "Yes," said Mr. Delahanty. "Yes, I'm afraid I was."

Americans Grab Paintbrushes as Volunteerism Surges

by Andrea Fine

1   For an increasing number of Americans, Martin Luther King Day is not a time of relaxation but a day to grab a broom or swab the floor of a cafeteria.

2   More than 10,000 people in Philadelphia alone volunteered to paint, sweep, or repair schools and streets around the area yesterday. Smaller groups in several cities—from Chicago to Charlotte, N.C., to San Diego—also used the holiday to clean up their neighborhoods.

3   The day of service is a testament to the spirit of Dr. King's legacy, but it also bears witness to something more. Polls show that volunteerism year-round is on the rise, as corporations and young people become more engaged in their communities. Indeed, the growth of the Philadelphia Day of Service—and others like it—is emblematic of an increased commitment to service nationwide.

4   "There has been more attention focused on volunteerism through events like the King Day of Service or the President's Summit on Volunteerism," says Nora Silver, director of The Volunteerism Project, a San Francisco-based initiative designed to strengthen and diversify public service.

5   When US Sen. Harris Wofford began the Philadelphia Day of Service in 1994, only about 1,000 turned out. Since then, the numbers have swelled, from 7,000 in 1997 to the anticipated 10,000 this year, making it the biggest Martin Luther King Day volunteer project in the United States.

6   It's a "commentary about volunteering in general," says Todd Bernstein, director of the Philadelphia Day of Service. "It's also a very strong statement about the King holiday and the shift toward finding meaningful ways to celebrate his life of action and helping others."

7   But the new face of volunteerism includes much more than people donating their time during a day off. "Corporations are [also] becoming increasingly involved, encouraging employees to participate in hands-on work, rather than simple gift-giving," says Ms. Silver. Schools, too, have begun "concentrating on service as a way to educate kids with experiential learning," she notes.

8   This service profile marks a departure from the old stereotype of the volunteer—the suburban housewife who had a weekly assignment in a local hospital, or with school PTAs or

libraries. Not only has the face of volunteerism shifted, there's also been a shift in the type of volunteer assignments people are seeking.

9   The most recent statistics, compiled in 1996 by the Gallup Organization, reported that 48.8 percent of the population was involved in volunteer activities for approximately 4.2 hours a week. "Many more people are wanting short-term volunteer opportunities," says Silver. "Businesses, cultural groups, and families seek a way of giving that is both short-term and [has an] impact."

10   As a result, there are now a number of organizations across the country that help prospective volunteers pinpoint areas where they can be most effective. At the end of the last decade, New York and Washington both had Cares organizations, which serve as liaison between volunteers and service opportunities. Now, there are 27 such organizations nationwide, accounting for the placement of about 100,000 volunteers.

11   "Groups like ours allow for more <u>diversification</u> in volunteer opportunities," says Lissa Hilsee, executive director of Philadelphia Cares.

12   Marguerite Redwine, who runs the Volunteer and Information Agency, an agency based in New Orleans that matches volunteers with projects, agrees. "We're able to match individual volunteers or corporations who might want 30 employees to participate in a weekend event to a volunteer assignment that is suited to their talent and schedule," she says.

13   For many, the most encouraging aspect of volunteerism today is the participation of young people. "Kids respond to volunteer opportunities," says Mr. Bernstein. "When they're given the chance to do something selfless for others and they receive acknowledgement for it, that's an empowering mechanism that promotes self-esteem and leadership."

14   He also notes that children are never too young to become involved. "We have projects in this year's Day of Service that attract kids as young as 6."

15   One organization, Do Something, is a national school-based organization founded jointly by actor Andrew Shue, formerly of "Melrose Place," and Martin Luther King III. Its goal is to inspire and mobilize young people to take action that will help strengthen their communities.

16   It uses the King holiday as a kick-off for its "Kindness and Justice Challenge"—a two-week initiative, beginning on Martin Luther King Day, which encourages children to perform acts of kindness in their communities and involves teachers and students in discussions of these values. The various Kindness and Justice acts completed are cited on a Web site, and schools are challenged to compete with one another for the most good deeds. Last year, students from more than 14,000 schools

participated. This year, more than 1.7 million students will be involved, according to program spokesman Rafe Bemporad.

17   "Students will receive recognition for the work they do," he says. "We believe if students can commit to two weeks of service, they can commit to a month. That becomes a year, then a year becomes a lifetime."

18   Bernstein, too, views the King Day of Service as a springboard to a year-round movement. "This really has become a 365-day-a-year project."

Build homes,
build a community
HOMES
FOR
ALL
CALL 555-HOME

**Use "Then He Goes Free," pages 2–8,
to answer questions 1–6.**

1 Based on the description in paragraph 34, which of the following is the correct definition of *olla*?

  A a heavy pottery water jar

  B a heavy wooden bench

  C a light plastic birdbath

  D a cement water fountain

Objective 1

2 What is paragraph 78 mainly about?

  A Cress describes her role in Edwin's injury.

  B Cress explains that she felt sorry for Edwin.

  C Cress admits that she likes Edwin.

  D The Delahantys learn what a "mush pot" is.

Objective 1

3 The details of the setting in paragraph 51 help to convey an atmosphere of —

  A anger

  B terror

  C optimism

  D gloom

Objective 2

4 What is the main conflict between the Delahantys and the Kibblers?

  A The Delahantys refuse to pay for Edwin's teeth.

  B The Kibblers falsely accuse Cress of injuring their son.

  C The Delahantys don't want to believe that their daughter is capable of violence.

  D The two families dislike one another.

Objective 2

5 Why do you think Cress chose Edwin first for her team?

  A She wanted to embarrass him in front of his classmates.

  B She felt protective of him.

  C She thought she had no choice.

  D She thought he might play better if he were chosen first.

Objective 3

6 What evidence leads you to believe that Cress might be interested in Edwin Kibbler?

  A She is shy when speaking of him.

  B She confesses that she knocked him down to get attention.

  C She expresses regret for what she has done.

  D She cares about preserving his dignity.

Objective 3

7 What is the correct definition of *diversification* as it is used in paragraph 11?

  A tolerance

  B challenge

  C formality

  D variety

Objective 1

8 The Day of Service was established as a way to —

  A give people looking for volunteer opportunities something to do

  B pay tribute to Dr. King by mobilizing people to act to improve their communities

  C do school maintenance work that had been neglected because of budget cutbacks

  D give young people a sense of responsibility and community service

Objective 1

9 Which of the following is NOT one of the new trends in volunteerism mentioned in the selection?

  A More young people are volunteering.

  B People are seeking more short-term volunteer opportunities.

  C Schoolchildren are being encouraged to donate their spare change to good causes.

  D Corporations are giving employees opportunities to do hands-on volunteer work.

Objective 1

10 Which quotation from the selection best summarizes the selection as a whole?

  A *Polls show that volunteerism year-round is on the rise, as corporations and young people become more engaged in their communities.*

  B *But the new face of volunteerism includes much more than people donating their time during a day off.*

  C *For many, the most encouraging aspect of volunteerism today is the participation of young people.*

  D *. . . [T]here are now a number of organizations across the country that help prospective volunteers pinpoint areas where they can be most effective.*

Objective 2

11 What generalization can be made from the references to the Day of Service, the President's Summit on Volunteerism, and the Kindness and Justice Challenge?

A Organizations that sponsor volunteer opportunities are overly focused on attracting publicity.

B Organized events are an effective way to attract participation in volunteer activities.

C More young people are taking part in volunteer projects than ever before.

D People won't take part in volunteer opportunities unless they are sure of receiving recognition.

Objective 3

12 Throughout the selection, the author uses statistics (number information) to —

A give information about the number of volunteers needed for projects nationwide

B show that volunteering is essential if communities are going to function properly

C persuade people that they should volunteer in their communities

D support the idea that more people are volunteering now than in the past

Objective 3

13 What is a common feature of "Then He Goes Free" and "Americans Grab Paintbrushes as Volunteerism Surges"?

A Both selections rely heavily on symbolism.

B Both selections include dialogue.

C Both selections have helping others as a theme.

D Both selections employ extended metaphors.

Objective 2

14 What characteristic does Cress Delahanty share with people who volunteer in their communities?

A stubbornness

B bravery

C a desire to make things better

D attention to detail

Objective 2

15 The purpose of this billboard is to —

A persuade people to purchase their own homes

B persuade people to volunteer for Homes for All

C explain how to become a volunteer for Homes for All

D explain how volunteering benefits the community

Objective 3

16 The billboard's underlying message is that —

A people can improve their communities by building homes for those in need

B building homes is an enjoyable pastime

C every person should have a home

D people should volunteer in organizations that will improve their communities

Objective 3

17   In "Then He Goes Free," what is the nature of the relationship between Cress Delahanty and Edwin Kibbler? Be sure to use evidence from the selection to support your answer.

Objective 2

18   Why do volunteer organizations emphasize the importance of getting young people involved in volunteer work? Be sure to use evidence from "Americans Grab Paintbrushes as Volunteerism Surges" to support your answer.

Objective 2

19   How do both "Then He Goes Free" and "Americans Grab Paintbrushes as Volunteerism Surges" show that people who are willing to make a sacrifice can benefit others? Be sure to use evidence from **both** selections to support your answer.

Objective 2

Writing Prompt

> Write a composition that explains how helping others can benefit the person giving help as much as it benefits those receiving help.

Respond to the writing prompt above on a separate sheet of paper. Think about the items in the box below as you write your composition.

REMEMBER TO

- write about the topic

- make your composition interesting and thoughtful

- make sure that each sentence adds to the reader's understanding of your composition

- state your ideas clearly

- include details to help the reader understand your ideas

- check your composition for problems with spelling, capitalization, punctuation, grammar, and sentence structure

Revising and Editing Passage 1 and Items

Sukura has written this report for a science course. She has asked you to proofread the report and offer suggestions for improvement. After you read Sukura's report, answer the multiple-choice questions that follow.

The Search for Intelligent Computers

(1) For decades people have been predicting that in the near future machines will be able to think like humans. (2) At one time, thinking machines were merely the stuff of science fiction. (3) The late Isaac Asimov, author of *I, Robot* and other books, pondered the consequences of machines who could think and perhaps even display other human characteristics, such as loyalty. (4) Despite all the imaginative stories about them, true thinking machines remain an element of fiction.

(5) Indeed, computers can do things that humans, but no other animals—can do. (6) Some people may point to computers as examples, of artificial intelligence. (7) In fact, there are many things, such as complex mathematical computations, that computers can do considerably faster and more accurately than people can. (8) In 1997, a computer—the IBM Deep Blue—beat a chess master, Garry Kasparov, for the first time. (9) But does performing mathematical computations or winning a chess match demonstrate intelligence?

(10) Most experts in the field think not; they would hold out for a higher standard. (11) In the 1950s, the British mathematician Alan Turing proposed a test which is now known as the Turing Test. (12) In the Turing Test, a human being serves as "the judge." (13) He poses the same question to a person and to a computer, without knowing which is which. (14) If the judge cannot determine which is which from the answers, the computer passes the test. (15) So far, computers have passed the test for some questions but will fail it for others. (16) Therefore, according to the experts, we do not yet have true artificial intelligence.

(17) Some experts in the field maintain that we will never have true artificial intelligence. (18) Computers, they insist, cannot hardly think in the same way that people do. (19) For example, the spellchecker on a computer's word-processing program can recognize a

misspelled word, but only by comparing it to tens of thousands of words in its word bank.
(20) This kind of clerical process, while applying quickness and efficiency, is not really
"thinking."

(21) In any case, the search continues.

1 What change, if any, should be made to
   sentence 3?

   A Change *who could think* to **that
   could think**

   B Delete the comma after *Isaac
   Asimov*

   C Change *other human characteristics*
   to **another human characteristic**

   D Make no change

Objective 6

2 What change, if any, should be made to
   sentence 5?

   A Delete the comma after *indeed* and
   add a colon

   B Change the comma after *humans* to
   a dash

   C Delete the dash after *animals*

   D Make no change

Objective 6

3 What change, if any, should be made to
   sentence 6?

   A Insert a comma after *people*

   B Change the word *to* to **at**

   C Delete the comma after *examples*

   D Make no change

Objective 6

4 What is the most effective way to
   improve the organization of the second
   paragraph (sentences 5–9)?

   A Move sentence 6 to the beginning of
   the paragraph

   B Delete sentence 7

   C Delete sentence 8

   D Move sentence 9 to the beginning of
   the paragraph

Objective 6

5 What change, if any, should be made in
   sentence 11?

   A Change *mathematician* to
   mathematition

   B Insert commas before and after *Alan
   Turing*

   C Add a comma after *test*

   D Make no change

Objective 6

6 The meaning of sentence 13 can be
   clarified by changing *He* to —

   A She

   B It

   C The judge

   D Turing

Objective 6

7 What is the most effective way to rewrite the ideas in sentence 14?

   A If the judge cannot tell which answer is from the computer and which answer is from the person, the computer passes the test.

   B If the answers cannot tell the judge which is the computer, the computer passes the test.

   C The computer passes the test when the judge cannot tell which is the computer.

   D The judge cannot determine which is the computer, so the computer passes the test.

Objective 6

8 What change, if any, should be made in sentence 15?

   A Delete the comma after *far*

   B Change *passed* to **past**

   C Change *will fail* to **have failed**

   D Make no change

Objective 6

9 What change, if any, should be made in sentence 18?

   A Delete the comma after *Computers*

   B Delete the comma after *insist*

   C Change *cannot hardly think* to **cannot think**

   D Change *that people do* to **as people do**

Objective 6

10 What is the most effective way to rewrite the idea in the last sentence?

   A In any case, the search for a better spellchecker continues.

   B In any case, the search for a true thinking machine continues.

   C The search continues, in any case, for computers that can convincingly defeat more chess champions.

   D So the search continues on for computers that can think.

Objective 6

Revising and Editing Passage 2 and Items

Brent has written this paper for a science class. He has asked you to proofread the paper and offer suggestions for improvement. After you read Brent's report, answer the multiple-choice questions that follow.

How Can the Woolly Adelgids Be Stopped?

(1) You may wonder what "adelgids" are. (2) Woolly adelgids are very small insects that have come to the United States from Asia. (3) What are they doing that needs to be stopped? (4) The answer to this question is taking us to the hemlock forests of the northeastern United States.

(5) Hemlock trees grow in thick stands in states along the Appalachian Mountains. (6) Usually along the banks of streams. (7) The hemlocks have a profound influence on the ecosystems that develop around them. (8) For one thing, the shade provided by the trees lowers the temperature of water in the streams. (9) The cooler water is ideal for trout and other creatures that cannot tollerate warm water. (10) Also, in the thick, damp hemlock canopy, where the leaves come together and block the sunlight, ferns, lichens, and mosses grow well. (11) A wide variety of animals also live there, such as salamanders, frogs, toads, and shrews.

(12) Woolly adelgids get their nourishment by poking through the tissue of the hemlock tree and sap out the tree's fluids. (13) The adelgids lay their little white eggs on the needles of hemlock trees. (14) As the insects develop, they attack the tree, hundreds of thousands of adelgids at a time. (15) The tree cannot nourish itself, so it dries up and dies. (16) The trees die and the entire ecosystem suffers as the habitat is destroyed.

(17) Releasing black ladybug beetles that will prey on adelgids is one effort to stop the adelgids from destroying hemlocks and is an experimental project. (18) The theory is that the ladybugs are the natural enemies of the adelgids, and thus protect the hemlock trees. (19) The results have been promising. (20) In some tests the ladybugs cut the adelgid population by about half. (21) In other tests, the ladybugs wiped out the adelgids completely. (22)

Experimental tests to reduce the adelgid population were conducted in Virginia and Connecticut in the late 1990s.

(23) If the adelgids are not controlled, big problems could lie ahead. (24) The adelgids seem to have moved about 30 miles per year since the 1950s through the areas of Virginia, North Carolina, New York, and New Jersey. (25) The fear is that the adelgids will spread like crazy as they get into longer and fuller hemlock stands.

1 What change, if any, should be made to sentence 4?

   A Insert a comma after *question*

   B Change *is taking* to **takes**

   C Change *northeastern* to **north eastern**

   D Make no change

Objective 6

2 What is the most effective way to combine the ideas in sentences 5 and 6?

   A Usually along the banks of streams, hemlock trees grow in thick stands in states along the Appalachian Mountains.

   B Hemlock trees grow in thick stands usually along the banks of streams in states along the Appalachian Mountains.

   C In states along the Appalachian Mountains usually along the banks of streams, hemlock trees grow in thick stands.

   D In states along the Appalachian Mountains, hemlock trees grow in thick stands, usually along the banks of streams.

Objective 6

3 What change, if any, should be made to sentence 9?

   A Change *cooler* to **coolest**

   B Change *cannot* to **can not**

   C Change *tollerate* to **tolerate**

   D Make no change

Objective 6

4 What change, if any, should be made in sentence 10?

   A Delete the comma after *thick*

   B Insert a comma after *damp*

   C Change the comma after *sunlight* to a colon

   D Make no change

Objective 6

5 What change should be made in sentence 12?

   A Change *their* to **they**

   B Change *through* to **thorough**

   C Change *sap* to **sapping**

   D Change *tree's* to **trees**

Objective 6

6 Which transition should be added to the beginning of sentence 16?

   A Consequently,

   B Instead,

   C Nevertheless,

   D Secondly,

Objective 6

7 What is the most effective way to rewrite sentence 17?

   A One effort to stop the adelgids from destroying hemlocks is releasing black ladybug beetles that will prey on adelgids and is an experimental project.

   B One effort to stop the adelgids from destroying hemlocks is an experimental project to release black ladybug beetles that will prey on adelgids.

   C One effort to stop the adelgids from destroying hemlocks: an experimental project releasing black ladybug beetles that will prey on adelgids.

   D Releasing black ladybug beetles that will prey on adelgids is an experimental project and it is one effort to stop the adelgids from destroying hemlocks.

Objective 6

8 What is the most effective way to improve the organization of the fourth paragraph (sentences 17–22)?

   A Delete sentence 18

   B Delete sentence 19

   C Move sentence 19 to the end of the paragraph

   D Move sentence 22 to the beginning of the paragraph

Objective 6

9 What change, if any, should be made in sentence 25?

   A Change *will spread* to **have spread**

   B Change *like crazy* to **even faster**

   C Change *fuller* to **fullest**

   D Make no change

Objective 6

10 Which of these sentences could be added to the end of the last paragraph (sentences 23–25) to support the ideas in that paragraph?

   A The hemlocks must be saved; bring in the ladybugs!

   B Scientists hope that the ladybug solution will be a safe and effective cure for the adelgid problem.

   C Everyone can help prevent the spread of adelgids by not using pesticides that kill ladybugs.

   D The pace of the moving adelgids is moving like an uncontrolled wildfire, killing everything in its path.

Objective 6

GRADE 11, PRACTICE TEST 1   ANSWER SHEET

Reading: Multiple-Choice Items

1 Ⓐ Ⓑ Ⓒ Ⓓ   5 Ⓐ Ⓑ Ⓒ Ⓓ   9 Ⓐ Ⓑ Ⓒ Ⓓ   13 Ⓐ Ⓑ Ⓒ Ⓓ
2 Ⓐ Ⓑ Ⓒ Ⓓ   6 Ⓐ Ⓑ Ⓒ Ⓓ   10 Ⓐ Ⓑ Ⓒ Ⓓ   14 Ⓐ Ⓑ Ⓒ Ⓓ
3 Ⓐ Ⓑ Ⓒ Ⓓ   7 Ⓐ Ⓑ Ⓒ Ⓓ   11 Ⓐ Ⓑ Ⓒ Ⓓ   15 Ⓐ Ⓑ Ⓒ Ⓓ
4 Ⓐ Ⓑ Ⓒ Ⓓ   8 Ⓐ Ⓑ Ⓒ Ⓓ   12 Ⓐ Ⓑ Ⓒ Ⓓ   16 Ⓐ Ⓑ Ⓒ Ⓓ

Reading: Open-Ended Items

17 ____

____

____

____

18 ____

____

____

____

19 ____

____

____

____

____

____

____

Writing:
Revising and Editing Passage 1 Items

1 Ⓐ Ⓑ Ⓒ Ⓓ		**6** Ⓐ Ⓑ Ⓒ Ⓓ
2 Ⓐ Ⓑ Ⓒ Ⓓ		**7** Ⓐ Ⓑ Ⓒ Ⓓ
3 Ⓐ Ⓑ Ⓒ Ⓓ		**8** Ⓐ Ⓑ Ⓒ Ⓓ
4 Ⓐ Ⓑ Ⓒ Ⓓ		**9** Ⓐ Ⓑ Ⓒ Ⓓ
5 Ⓐ Ⓑ Ⓒ Ⓓ		**10** Ⓐ Ⓑ Ⓒ Ⓓ

Revising and Editing Passage 2 Items

1 Ⓐ Ⓑ Ⓒ Ⓓ		**6** Ⓐ Ⓑ Ⓒ Ⓓ
2 Ⓐ Ⓑ Ⓒ Ⓓ		**7** Ⓐ Ⓑ Ⓒ Ⓓ
3 Ⓐ Ⓑ Ⓒ Ⓓ		**8** Ⓐ Ⓑ Ⓒ Ⓓ
4 Ⓐ Ⓑ Ⓒ Ⓓ		**9** Ⓐ Ⓑ Ⓒ Ⓓ
5 Ⓐ Ⓑ Ⓒ Ⓓ		**10** Ⓐ Ⓑ Ⓒ Ⓓ

Grade 11

TAKS Practice Test 2

- **Reading Selections, Visual Representation, and Items**
- **Writing Prompt**
- **Revising and Editing Passage 1 and Items**
- **Revising and Editing Passage 2 and Items**

Reading Selections and Items

DIRECTIONS

Read these selections and the visual representation. When you are finished, answer the questions that follow.

Miss Brill

by Katherine Mansfield

1   Although it was so brilliantly fine—the blue sky powdered with gold and great spots of light like white wine splashed over the Jardins Publiques[1]—Miss Brill was glad that she had decided on her fur. The air was motionless, but when you opened your mouth, there was just a faint chill, like a chill from a glass of iced water before you sip, and now and again a leaf came drifting—from nowhere, from the sky. Miss Brill put up her hand and touched her fur. Dear little thing! It was nice to feel it again. She had taken it out of its box that afternoon, shaken out the moth powder, given it a good brush and rubbed the life back into the dim little eyes. "What has been happening to me?" said the sad little eyes. Oh, how sweet it was to see them snap at her again from the red eiderdown![2] . . . But the nose, which was of some black composition, wasn't at all firm. It must have had   a knock somehow. Never mind—a little dab of black sealing wax when the time came—when it was absolutely necessary . . . Little rogue! Yes, she really felt like that about it. Little rogue biting it's tail just by her left ear. She could have taken it off and laid it on her lap and stroked it. She felt a tingling in her hands and arms, but that came from walking, she supposed. And when she breathed, something light and sad—no, not sad, exactly—something gentle seemed to move in her bosom.

2   There were a number of people out this afternoon, far more than last Sunday. And the band sounded louder and gayer. That was because the Season had begun. For although the band played all the year round on Sundays, out of season it was never the same. It was like someone playing with only the family to listen; it didn't care how it played if there weren't any strangers present. Wasn't the conductor wearing a new coat, too? She was sure it was new. He scraped with his foot and flapped his arms like a rooster about to crow, and the bandsmen sitting in the green rotunda[3] blew out their cheeks and glared at the music. Now there came a little "flutey" bit—very pretty!—a little chain of bright drops. She was sure it would be repeated. It was; she lifted her head and smiled.

Reading notes

---

1. Jardins Publiques: French for "Public Gardens."
2. eiderdown: bed quilt stuffed with down from an eider duck.
3. rotunda: a circular structure, usually covered by a dome.

3   Only two people shared her "special" seat: a fine old man in a velvet coat, his hands clasped over a huge carved walking stick, and a big old woman, sitting upright, with a roll of knitting on her embroidered apron. They did not speak. This was disappointing, for Miss Brill always looked forward to the conversation. She had become really quite expert, she thought, at listening as though she didn't listen, as sitting in other people's lives just for a minute while they talked round her.

4   She glanced, sideways, at the old couple. Perhaps they would go soon. Last Sunday, too, hadn't been as interesting as usual. An Englishman and his wife, he wearing a dreadful Panama hat and she button boots. And she'd gone on the whole time about how she ought to wear spectacles; she knew she needed them; but that it was no good getting any; they'd be sure to break and they'd never keep on. And he'd been so patient. He's suggested everything—gold rims, the kind that curved round your ears, little pads inside the bridge. No, nothing would please her. "They'll always be sliding down my nose!" Miss Brill had wanted to shake her.

5   The old people sat on the bench, still as statues. Never mind, there was always the crowd to watch. To and fro, in front of the flower beds and the band rotunda, the couples and groups paraded, stopped to talk, to greet, to buy a handful of flowers from the old beggar who had his tray fixed to the railings. Little children ran among them, swooping and laughing; little boys with big white silk bows under their chins, little girls, little French dolls, dressed up in velvet and lace. And sometimes a tiny staggerer came suddenly rocking into the open from under the trees, stopped, stared, as suddenly sat down "flop," until its small high-stepping mother, like a young hen, rushed scolding to its rescue. Other people sat on the benches and green chairs, but they were nearly always the same, Sunday after Sunday, and—Miss Brill had often noticed—there was something funny about nearly all of them. They were odd, silent, nearly all old, and from the way they stared they looked as though they'd just come from dark little rooms or even—even cupboards!

6   Behind the rotunda the slender trees with yellow leaves down drooping, and through them just a line of sea, and beyond the blue sky with gold-veined clouds.

7   Tum-tum-tum tiddle-um! tiddle-um! tum tiddley-um tum ta! blew the band.

8   Two young girls in red came by and two young soldiers in blue met them, and they laughed and paired and went off arm in arm. Two peasant women with funny straw hats passed, gravely, leading beautiful smoke-colored donkeys. A cold, pale nun hurried by. A beautiful woman came along and dropped her bunch of violets, and a little boy ran after to hand them to her, and she took them and threw them away as if they'd been poisoned. Dear me! Miss Brill didn't know whether to admire

that or not! And now an ermine toque[4] and a gentleman in gray met just in front of her. He was tall, stiff, dignified, and she was wearing the ermine toque she'd bought when her hair was yellow. Now everything, her hair, her face, even her eyes, was the same color as the shabby ermine, and her hand, in its cleaned glove, lifted to dab her lips, was a tiny yellowish paw. Oh, she was so pleased to see him—delighted! She rather thought they were going to meet that afternoon. She described where she'd been—everywhere, here, there, along by the sea. The day was so charming—didn't he agree? And wouldn't he, perhaps? . . . But he shook his head, lighted a cigarette, slowly breathed a great deep puff into her face, and, even while she was still talking and laughing, flicked the match away and walked on. The ermine toque was alone; she smiled more brightly than ever. But even the band seemed to know what she was feeling and played more softly, played tenderly, and the drum beat, "The Brute! The Brute!" over and over. What would she do? What was going to happen now? But as Miss Brill wondered, the ermine toque turned, raised her hand as though she'd seen someone else, much nicer, just over there, and pattered away. And the band changed again and played more quickly, more gayly than ever, and the old couple on Miss Brill's seat got up and marched away, and such a funny old man with long whiskers hobbled along in time to the music and was nearly knocked over by four girls walking abreast.

9   Oh, how fascinating it was! How she enjoyed it! How she loved sitting here, watching it all! It was like a play. It was exactly like a play. Who could believe the sky at the back wasn't painted? But it wasn't till a little brown dog trotted on solemn and then slowly trotted off, like a little "theater" dog, a little dog that had been drugged, that Miss Brill discovered what it was that made it so exciting. They were all on the stage. They weren't only the audience, not only looking on; they were acting. Even she had a part and came every Sunday. No doubt somebody would have noticed if she hadn't been there; she was part of the performance after all. How strange she'd never thought of it like that before! And yet it explained why she made such a point of starting from home at just the same time each week—so as not to be late for the performance—and it also explained why she had quite a queer, shy feeling at telling her English pupils how she spent her Sunday afternoons. No wonder! Miss Brill nearly laughed out loud. She was on the stage. She thought of the old invalid gentleman to whom she read the newspaper four afternoons a week while he slept in the garden. She had got quite used to the frail head on the cotton pillow, the hollowed eyes, the open mouth and the high pinched nose. If he'd been dead she mightn't have noticed for weeks; she wouldn't have minded. But suddenly he knew he was having the

___
4. toque: a close-fitting hat.

paper read to him by an actress! "An actress!" The old head lifted; two points of light quivered in the old eyes. "An actress—are ye?" And Miss Brill smoothed the newspaper as though it were the manuscript of her part and said gently: "Yes, I have been an actress for a long time."

10   The band had been having a rest. Now they started again. And what they played was warm, sunny, yet there was just a faint chill—a something, what was it?—not sadness—no, not sadness—a something that made you want to sing. The tune lifted, lifted, the light shone; and it seemed to Miss Brill that in another moment all of them, all the whole company, would begin singing. The young ones, the laughing ones who were moving together, they would begin, and the men's voices, very resolute and brave, would join them. And then she too, she too, and the others on the benches—they would come in with a kind of accompaniment—something low, that scarcely rose or fell, something so beautiful—moving . . . And Miss Brill's eyes filled with tears and she looked smiling at all the other members of the company. Yes, we understand, we understand, she thought—though what they understood she didn't know.

11   Just at that moment a boy and a girl came and sat down where the old couple had been. They were beautifully dressed; they were in love. The hero and heroine, of course, just arrived from his father's yacht. And still soundlessly singing, still with that trembling smile, Miss Brill prepared to listen.

12   "No, not now," said the girl. "Not here, I can't."

13   "But why? Because of that stupid old thing at the end there?" asked the boy. "Why does she come here at all—who wants her? Why doesn't she keep her silly old mug at home?"

14   "It's her fu-fur which is so funny," giggled the girl. "It's exactly like a fried whiting."[5]

15   "Ah, be off with you!" said the boy in an angry whisper. Then: "Tell me, ma petite chérie[6]—"

16   "No, not here," said the girl. "Not *yet.*"

17   On her way home she usually bought a slice of honey-cake at the baker's. It was her Sunday treat. Sometimes there was an almond in her slice, sometimes not. It made a great difference. If there was an almond it was like carrying home a tiny present—a surprise—something that might very well not have been there. She hurried on the almond Sundays and struck the match for the kettle in a quite dashing way.

18   But today she passed the baker's by, climbed the stairs, went into the little dark room—her room like a cupboard—and sat

5. whiting: a fish.
6. ma petite chérie: French for "my little darling."

down on the red eiderdown. She sat there for a long time. The box that the fur came out of was on the bed. She unclasped the necklet quickly; quickly without looking, laid it inside. But when she put the lid on she thought she heard something crying.

Seize the World

by Peter Potterfield

1   **On a cold December morning, under the 24-hour daylight of the Antarctic summer,** Californian Betty Platero, 62, climbed down the steps on the ice-hardened hull of a chartered converted Russian research vessel. Scrambling into a rubber Zodiac boat, she prepared for a rough ride through breaking surf toward a beach on South Georgia island. After landing, she found herself on a hill rising above an ineffably wild and pristine environment, gazing down at a sight few humans have enjoyed: more than 250,000 King penguins in full summer plumage, assembled in a remote rookery for their elaborate annual mating ritual. As she recorded the scene with her camera, Platero breathed in the salty air of the cold South Atlantic Ocean and relished the deep satisfaction of being in one of the world's wildest places.

2   **Although not her first—or last—adventure,** it was a special moment for Platero. After 31 years of teaching junior high and high school students, she has, since 1995, aggressively pursued her companion enthusiasms of photography, wildlife, and travel. She has embarked on journeys to see polar bears in northern Canada, orangutans in Indonesia, lions in Africa, and frost-encrusted buffalo in a Yellowstone winter. But that day on South Georgia, surrounded by glaciers and mountains, elephant seals and penguins, was a symbol to Platero of how rich her life had become through her ongoing <u>quest</u> to fulfill her passions.

3   **Whatever the desired experience**—a landing in Antarctica, a trek into the Grand Canyon, or a bicycle trip through the French countryside—going it on your own is no longer necessary. The latest figures show that at least 8,000 outfitters in the United States alone can satisfy your yen for excitement. According to the World Travel and Tourism Council, adventure is the fastest growing segment of the travel industry today, with more than 98 million adults pursuing a challenging experience in just the past five years alone.

4   **"The very definition of adventure travel has changed over the past several decades,"** says Richard Bangs, a founding partner of Mountain Travel-Sobek, one of the oldest and largest operators in the field. "In the early days, in the '60s, there was a very small client base for this business—mostly well-heeled

professionals who wanted lots of adventure and didn't mind taking serious risks or being uncomfortable doing it. The trips were expensive and full of unknowns and bad surprises. But the gradual shift toward 'soft' adventure in the mid-'80s opened the business to a larger population of clients who wanted something challenging but also demanded good planning and a relative degree of comfort."

5   **It's no accident that the concept of adventure became a mainstream phenomenon in the 20th century.** Modern life has stripped away many of the physical challenges that once were inherent in human existence. That void creates an unfulfilled need.

6   **"The desire to experience is important in today's virtual world,"** says Dawn Beckley, operations director for Alpine Ascents International, a travel company specializing in mountain climbing. "People can lose touch with their sense of physical purpose, and climbing is a way for those people to feel strong. To strive for something difficult, to go beyond what's called for in everyday life, becomes empowering and carries with it not just a physical sense of accomplishment but a spiritual one. The impact goes far beyond the experience itself. A real adventure stays with you. It becomes a part of who you are."

7   **More than a visit to a foreign city, the excitement of a serious adrenaline rush lingers.** For many people, adventure, once tasted, becomes addictive.

8   **"Lifestyles have changed,"** says Bud Davis, founder of the International Adventure Travel and Outdoor Show, the leading industry trade show. "Many people aren't content anymore to be beach potatoes and fry in the sun. Add to that a genuine concern about vanishing wilderness and the desire to get out in the magnificent outdoors before it disappears, and you've got the drive behind the growth in adventure travel."

9   **Bangs is a case in point.** Now 49 and editor-at-large for Microsoft's Expedia.com online travel site, he had, as a kid growing up in suburban Washington, D.C., an innate yearning for risk, and in his late teens he was seduced by the allure of fast rivers. One day he bought a cheap rubber raft and launched himself down the Little Falls rapids on the Potomac River. Submerged rocks soon ripped the bottom out of his raft and he almost drowned. But Bangs was electrified with excitement, and that epiphany led him to take a summer job as a guide on the Colorado River. "I was just blown away," he recalls. "Running

the canyon was beautiful, and the people who came along were incredible. In those days, it was only the rare person who would take a trip like that."

10   **His appetite whetted, Bangs upped the ante by heading to Ethiopia,** where there were rivers so wild that they had never before been run. His intent was to take a year off between graduation from Northwestern University and graduate school, a "last yahoo," as he puts it. But a dark, forbidding river called the Omo, full of crocodiles, poisonous snakes, lethal insects, and deadly rapids changed all that. After weeks in uncharted wilderness, he and his small band of companions ran out of food and had to abort the trip. They were in danger of starving when they stumbled out of the jungle onto a remote airstrip, and salvation.

11   **"The experience was so remarkable that I couldn't accept the idea of going back to normal life after that,"** he says. "There was such a richness to the adventures, everything seemed young and new, and the exotic sights and smells and languages just swept me away. I came home determined to see if I could make a living doing this."

12   **After that trip, Bangs and a friend founded Sobek,** named for the ancient Egyptian crocodile god. "When you try to define adventure," he says, "the only definition that makes sense is that it's more mental and emotional than anything else. When you challenge yourself, you learn from it and come back changed, with new strength and understanding."

13   **The transformative power of adventure is well-known to Keith and Antje Gunnar.** This couple from Whidbey Island, Washington, surrendered to their love of the outdoors when they first met 40 years ago, before there was an industry to cater to it. Keith put together a 20-day trek through the Himalayas of Nepal. No information was available on the area because no other Westerners had ever traveled this trekking route before, so Keith charted a course from Gorkha to Pokhara using the only resource he had: maps.

14   **The journey led them through valleys and villages, and eventually into the high rhododendron forests** on the lower slopes of the range. At one 15,000-foot pass, however, the Gunnars realized they were lost. Two of their Sherpa guides scouted a route they hoped would bring them out of the mountains, and eventually the small party descended out of the clouds to astonish a small village whose residents had never seen

a trekking party before. The Gunnars weren't sure what kind of reception they would get.

15 **They had nothing to fear.** The Nepalis greeted them warmly, adorned them with garlands of marigolds, and celebrated the occasion with an epic party. Keith and Antje were the guests of honor, plied all night with a potent distilled beverage called rakshi, and entertained with nonstop dancing and singing. "We must have seemed like aliens descending from the sky," Keith says.

16 **An expectation of wonderful moments has inspired the Gunnars** to pursue a life wholly given over to their first love—travel. "We decided not to have kids because we wanted to keep our freedom and be able to play," says Keith. "I even turned down a job as vice president of an aircraft company because I knew I wouldn't be able to travel. Instead, we were able to derive income from the photos we took while traveling to wild, remote places."

17 **When they met in 1960, Keith was working as an engineer** specializing in aircraft windshields for Boeing in Seattle, and German-born Antje was a Boeing liaison for Lufthansa. The airline connection made worldwide travel possible for them at a fraction of published fares. "We could fly to Alaska for $15," Keith recalls. "We once flew to New Delhi for $98. We sometimes got a ride on delivery flights to Europe. There were no limits in those days."

18 **A seminal moment of sorts came in the late '70s** when a new magazine, *Adventure Travel,* sent the Gunnars to Africa for a month to photograph wildlife safaris. The mere existence of such a magazine proved that the adventure-travel industry was coming into its own. The world was beginning to catch up with the Gunnars. The emergence of a service industry only fueled the couple's passion, and their pace of travel increased in the '80s and '90s to include more exotic destinations: Russia, Antarctica, remote Scandinavian archipelagos, the North Pole—all commercial offerings. Says Keith, stocky and strong at 71, five years older than Antje: "I don't think there's anywhere in the world you can't go to just by picking up the phone. That's the big difference from the '60s to today."

19 **For New Englander Sal Pomponi, the urge for adventure was awakened in midlife** and driven by a sudden passion for mountain climbing. Already well-traveled in his career as a systems engineer, Pomponi had also lived abroad. "Just before

my 50th birthday I did a mental review of my life," he says. "I had an extremely rewarding and satisfying career. I had a wonderful family. I had traveled extensively. I couldn't find a lot to wish for, but nevertheless I set two goals for myself: I would run a marathon and I would do an expedition climb."

20 **He did the marathon that year,** but orchestrating the climbing expedition took longer. His love of the mountains had already been nurtured by camping trips into the White Mountains of New Hampshire with his wife and children. By the early '80s, his grown son Marco had introduced him to the sport of rock climbing. Business trips to Tokyo had given him the opportunity to climb in the Japanese Alps. He was, in his own words, "really smitten by the beauty and exhilaration of mountaineering." He began to climb in earnest.

21 **Pomponi, 70 this year, can now look back on the past 20 years with an impressive résumé.** He has climbed the highest peaks on five of seven continents, including Aconcagua in South America, McKinley in North America, and Kilimanjaro in Africa. All ascents were made after his 60th birthday.

22 **"Climbing appeals to me on many levels,"** he says. "I like to push myself mentally and physically, and climbing demands that. It's a proven way to decompress from the tension of everyday life. Mountaineering has a way of putting life back into perspective for me because life is pretty simple on the mountain."

23 **But mountaineering is also dangerous,** and Pomponi knew he could not expect to climb as aggressively as he does without incident. Finally, one day the odds caught up with him. He was high on Ama Dablam, a 22,350-foot peak in the Khumbu Valley of Nepal, when he stepped to one side to check a piece of equipment. As he did so, a boulder dislodged from high above and roared past the spot where he had been standing. It struck the climber behind Pomponi, crushing his leg.

24 **It took Pomponi and his companions three days to get the injured climber down** to where he could be evacuated by helicopter. "Fortunately," says Pomponi, "everything turned out well. But I still wonder what that boulder could have done to me if I hadn't stopped when I did."

25 **If there is an ambition for him that remains unfulfilled,** it is to climb an 8,000-meter (26,240-foot) peak. There are only 14

such mountains in the world, and his previous attempt to climb one—a venture on Mount Everest in 1993—was unsuccessful. But he is undaunted. "I hope to keep climbing," he says. "If you get trapped into defining your actions and ambitions solely by age, you're going to miss a lot of opportunities to enjoy life."

ACCOMPLISH!
The Magazine of Individual Achievement
COVER STORY:
MEET CHARLES SCHWEITZER, 78
CHAMPION SENIOR MOUNTAIN BIKER
HIGH SCHOOL STUDENTS WHO ARE MAKING A DIFFERENCE
QUIZ: ARE YOU ON TRACK TO MEET YOUR GOALS?

1 Look at the following sentence from the story.

The young ones, the laughing ones who were moving together, they would begin, and the men's voices, very resolute and brave, would join them.

Based on its context, *resolute* probably means —

A steady and determined

B calm and insistent

C joyous and lilting

D wavering and fearful

Objective 1

2 Why does Miss Brill go to the park every Sunday?

A To hear the band play

B To exercise for her health

C To watch and listen to the people there

D To act in a theatrical performance

Objective 1

3 The remarks made by the young girl and boy make Miss Brill realize that —

A she is not an actress in a performance

B she is pathetic and ridiculous

C she is very popular with everyone at the park

D people know when she listens to their conversations

Objective 2

4 In what way are the observations Miss Brill makes about the old people ironic?

A Some of the old people used to be her friends.

B The "old people" are younger than she is.

C She learns that the old people are having conversations about her.

D She doesn't realize that those observations also apply to her.

Objective 2

5 Which of the following passages from the story contains an example of metaphor?

A *"What has been happening to me?" said the little eyes.*

B *He scraped with his foot and flapped his arms like a rooster about to crow.*

C *. . . little girls, little French dolls, dressed up in velvet and lace.*

D *Two peasant women with funny straw hats passed, gravely, leading beautiful smoke-colored donkeys.*

Objective 2

6 The fact that Miss Brill habitually
observes people and listens to their
conversations shows that —

A Miss Brill is an expert at
understanding other people.

B Miss Brill's life is lonely and empty.

C Miss Brill is afraid to talk with other
people.

D Miss Brill is planning to share her
observations with her students.

Objective 3

7 Which of these is the best summary of the selection?

A Adventure travel can be dangerous and life-threatening. Sal Pomponi was almost killed by a boulder while climbing a peak in Nepal. Instead, the boulder crushed the leg of a climber just below him. Pomponi and his companions then risked their lives by taking three days to help the hurt climber to safety. Even though it was a dangerous experience, Pomponi anticipates more climbing trips.

B Because the fast-growing adventure travel industry has become more mainstream, older people like Betty Platero can visit places that they once only dreamed of visiting. One experience common to those who partake in adventure travel is a sense of having been transformed. Richard Bangs, for example, found that he couldn't go back to everyday life after his adventure in Ethiopia. He later founded a successful adventure-travel outfitter.

C With the adventure-travel industry booming, finding a job as an outfitter is easy. A typical operator might plan and execute trips to Kilimanjaro in Africa, the Grand Canyon in the United States, or South Georgia island in the Antarctic. Since people have more time and money than they had in the past, business is unfailingly profitable.

D People at all ages crave adventure. Whether it's a retired school teacher or a former aircraft engineer, people are seeking ways to celebrate life that don't involve sunning themselves on a tropical island. Even if the travel involves dangerous or life-threatening situations, people are willing to take these risks if it means they will have a good time and a unique experience.

Objective 1

8 Paragraphs 5 and 6 are mainly about —

A the role that adventure travel plays in modern life

B the types of trips available to adventure travelers

C how adventure travel can be physically challenging

D how adventure travel can be a religious experience for some people

Objective 1

9 In paragraph 2, the use of the word *quest* helps the reader understand that people view adventure travel as —

A necessary, but painful

B a way to pass the time

C important to their happiness

D an easy way to see the world

Objective 3

10 Which quotation from the selection best summarizes the author's view on aging and adventure?

A *Modern life has stripped away many of the physical challenges that once were inherent in human existence. That void creates an unfulfilled need.*

B *For many people, adventure, once tasted, becomes addictive.*

C *Says Keith, stocky and strong at 71 . . . "I don't think there's anywhere in the world you can't go to just by picking up the phone. . . ."*

D *"If you get trapped into defining your actions and ambitions solely by age, you're going to miss a lot of opportunities to enjoy life."*

Objective 3

11 The author develops this selection by —

A describing remote places one might visit on a travel adventure

B comparing the different adventure-travel outfitters available

C recounting the travel experiences of four different people

D offering solutions to the problem of what to do during retirement

Objective 3

12 The author uses boldfaced type at the beginning of each paragraph to —

A introduce the topic of each paragraph so a reader can scan for meaning

B emphasize important points

C summarize the main ideas in the article

D help readers with poor eyesight see the paragraph breaks

Objective 3

13 Both Miss Brill and the travelers featured in "Seize the World" experience a change in perspective because they —

A are older and wiser

B have an experience that changes the way they think about life

C visit a place that they enjoy

D have a conversation with someone that changes their outlook

Objective 3

14 The difference in the time periods in which the two selections are set affects —

A how older people are portrayed in each selection

B the figures of speech in each selection

C the length of each selection

D the setting of each selection

Objective 3

15 The reader would expect this magazine's articles to focus on —

A high-school students who excel in academics

B a wide variety of topics, such as current events, sports, and news

C stories that interest older people

D noteworthy deeds by people from all walks of life

Objective 3

16 What underlying message is conveyed by the picture on the magazine's cover?

A older people like to ride mountain bikes

B older people can be healthy, fit athletes

C mountain bikers like to show off their muscles

D mountain bikers should always wear safety equipment

Objective 3

17 In "Miss Brill," how does Miss Brill's view of herself change from the beginning of the story to the end? Be sure to use evidence from the selection to support your answer.

Objective 2

18 In "Seize the World," how have the featured individuals' attitudes about life been shaped by their adventure-travel experiences? Be sure to use evidence from the selection to support your answer.

Objective 3

19 How is Miss Brill like or different from the older people described in the article "Seize the World"? Be sure to use evidence from **both** selections to support your answer.

Objective 2

Writing Prompt

Write a composition that explains how a person's experiences shape who he or she is.

Respond to the writing prompt above on a separate sheet of paper. Think about the items in the box below as you write your composition.

REMEMBER TO

- write about the topic

- make your composition interesting and thoughtful

- make sure that each sentence adds to the reader's understanding of your composition

- state your ideas clearly

- include details to help the reader understand your ideas

- check your composition for problems with spelling, capitalization, punctuation, grammar, and sentence structure

Revising and Editing Passage 1 and Items

Anish has written this paper for a history class. He has asked you to proofread the paper and offer suggestions for improvement. After you read Anish's report, answer the multiple-choice questions that follow.

Marie Antoinette

(1) One of the most despised figures in history was the french queen Marie Antoinette. (2) Her mother was Maria Theresa, a very popular empress who ruled over much of what is now Austria and Hungary. (3) Maria Theresa and her husband, Francis Stephen, who was the duke of Lorraine, had sixteen children. (4) Maria Theresa and Francis Stephen ruled during very troubled times but was able to rally their loyal subjects to help defend their lands against outside invaders and other problems.

(5) Marie Antoinette, on the other hand, received no such loyalty from her subjects she didn't deserve it. (6) Married at a young age to the crown prince of France, Marie became queen four years later when her husband was crowned Louis XVI. (7) However, she was a poorly educated queen who cared little for the important affairs of state. (8) She found these affairs quite boring. (9) Instead, she indulged herself with frivolous pleasures, including horse races, gambling, and extravagant parties.

(10) When experienced and capable ministers in the French government urged the king to cut back on reckless spending and indiscreet behavior, Marie often convinced her husband to dismiss them. (11) The nation fell deeper and deeper into financial crisis, while the parties and the behavior at the royal court became more and more outrageous.

(12) According to one famous anecdote, when she was told about a severe lack of bread among the masses, she is reported to have replied sarcastically, Then let them eat cake. (13) Marie herself was extremely unpopular with the common people and rumors abounded about her insensitivity. (14) Although this story may not have been true people believed it.

(15) They also believed other stories about the queen's shortcomings, including stories that she was selling France's military secrets to other nations.

(16) Shortly after the French Revolution began in 1789, Marie further angered the populace by convincing her husband to call out troops to protect the palace. (17) Finally, the royal couple were arrested as they tried to flee in disguise. (18) Rather than compromise with the revolutionaries, Marie plotted to receive military aid from her brother, Joseph II of Austria. (19) All her plots failed, and eventually her and her husband were both executed by angry mobs of revolutionaries.

1 What change, if any, should be made to sentence 1?

A Insert a comma after *history*

B Change *french* to **French**

C Change *queen* to **Queen**

D Make no change

Objective 6

2 What change, if any, should be made in sentence 4?

A Insert a comma after *times*

B Change *was* to **were**

C Change *their* to **they**

D Make no change

Objective 6

3 What is the most effective way to rewrite sentence 5?

A Marie Antoinette, on the other hand, received no such loyalty from her subjects, nor did she deserve it.

B Marie Antoinette, on the other hand, received no such loyalty from her subjects, she didn't deserve it.

C Because she didn't deserve it, Marie Antoinette, on the other hand, received no such loyalty from her subjects.

D On the other hand, Marie Antoinette received no such loyalty from her subjects she didn't deserve it.

Objective 6

4 What is the most effective way to combine sentences 7 and 8?

A However, she was a poorly educated queen who cared little for the important affairs of state, she found these affairs quite boring.

B Finding these affairs quite boring, however, she was a poorly educated queen who cared little for the important affairs of state.

C However, she was a poorly educated queen who cared little for the important affairs of state, which she found quite boring.

D However, finding these affairs quite boring, she was a poorly educated queen who cared little for the important affairs of state.

Objective 6

5 What change, if any, should be made in sentence 9?

A Change *she* to **her**

B Change *indulged* to **indulging**

C Insert a comma after *including*

D Make no change

Objective 6

6 What transition should be added to the beginning of sentence 11?

A Thus,

B Before,

C Finally,

D Nevertheless,

Objective 6

7 What change should be made in sentence 12?

   A Change *severe* to **seveer**

   B Change *is reported* to **has been reported**

   C Delete the comma after *sarcastically*

   D Change *Then let them eat cake.* to **"Then let them eat cake."**

Objective 6

8 What change, if any, should be made in sentence 14?

   A Insert a comma after *Although*

   B Insert a comma after *been*

   C Insert a comma after *true*

   D Make no change

Objective 6

9 What is the most effective way to improve the organization of the fourth paragraph (sentences 12–15)?

   A Move sentence 13 to the beginning of the paragraph

   B Delete sentence 13

   C Delete sentence 14

   D Move sentence 14 so that it follows sentence 12

Objective 6

10 What change, if any, should be made in sentence 19?

   A Delete the comma after *failed*

   B Change *eventually* to **eventualy**

   C Change *her* to **she**

   D Make no change

Objective 6

Revising and Editing Passage 2 and Items

Susan has written this story for a language arts class. She has asked you to proofread the story and offer suggestions for improvement. After you read Susan's story, answer the multiple-choice questions that follow.

Christina's New Job

(1) When she put down the phone, Christina's hands were shaking. (2) She couldn't believe her luck. (3) She had just been told that she would spend the summer working as a member of a white-water rafting crew in the Grand Canyon! (4) Immediately Christina began to imagine the glamerous adventures she would have in the next three months.

(5) Before she knew it, Christina was standing on the banks of the powerful Colorado River. (6) She spent four days training for her new job with Marty Michaels, the guide who would lead Christina and a group of tourists on a week-long trip down the river. (7) She had patiently sorted gear, planned menus, went shopping for supplies, and waterproofed the special bags that would hold the supplies. (8) She had been an attentive student. (9) She secretly wondered if all her responsibilities would be so mundane.

(10) The first morning of the journey down the river was calm and uneventful, the boat making its way swiftly and smoothly through the coffee-brown water. (11) Suddenly, as the raft approached the first run of white-water rapids, it makes an unexpected, twisting turn in the current. (12) "Everybody hang on!" Marty yelled. (13) He desperately tried to swerve the raft away from a large boulder jutting out in the middle of the river, but the stern struck the rock. (14) A loud grinding noise came from the motor.

(15) "Propeller's smashed!" yelled Marty over the roar of the rapids. (16) "We'll have to let the current push us over to the riverbank." (18) The passengers clutched the sides of the raft and stared, wide-eyed and silent, at Christina and Marty as the raft drifted to the rocky bank that edged the river. (19) "Come on, Christina", Marty called when they reached the bank, "climb out onto that big rock and hang onto this rope while I change the motor."

(20) Marty quickly replaced the smashed motor. (21) Just as Christina breathed a sigh of relief, another twist of the current struck the raft broadside and jerked the rope from her hands. (22) She stared in disbelief as the raft swiftly flowed downstream, leaving her stranded on it. (23) The shock of finding herself stranded was balanced only by her embarrassment at losing her hold on the rope.

(24) That evening Christina was in a reflective mood. (25) Christina wondered what type of job she would have next summer. (26) She felt good about the work she had done throughout the afternoon, and she had acquired a new respect for the power of nature. (27) By the time dinner was over, Christina had made a rule for herself, focus on doing the job instead of on the adventure.

1 What change, if any, should be made in sentence 4?

   A Add a comma after *began*

   B Change *glamerous* to **glamorous**

   C Change *would have* to **would be having**

   D Make no change

Objective 6

2 What change should be made in sentence 7?

   A Add commas before and after *patiently*

   B Change *planned* to **planning**

   C Change *went shopping* to **shopped**

   D Change *bags that* to **bags who**

Objective 6

3 What is the most effective way to combine sentences 8 and 9?

   A She had been an attentive student, but she secretly wondered if all her responsibilities would be so mundane.

   B She secretly wondered if all her responsibilities would be so mundane, because she had been an attentive student.

   C She had been an attentive student and she secretly wondered if all her responsibilities would be so mundane.

   D She had been an attentive student, she secretly wondered if all her responsibilities would be so mundane.

Objective 6

4 What change, if any, should be made in sentence 11?

   A Delete the comma after *Suddenly*

   B Change *makes* to **made**

   C Change *unexpected* to **unexpectedly**

   D Make no change

Objective 6

5 What change, if any, should be made in sentence 19?

   A Change *Christina",* to **Christina,"**

   B Delete the comma after *bank*

   C Change *onto* to **on to**

   D Make no change

Objective 6

6 Which of these sentences could be added to the end of the fourth paragraph (sentences 15–19) to support the ideas in that paragraph?

   A None of those passengers would ever go white-water rafting again.

   B Everyone Christina knew would be proud of her quick reaction to the problem.

   C Christina's job had just become more interesting.

   D It had been a peaceful beginning to Christina's white-water rafting experience.

Objective 6

7 What transition should be added to the
beginning of sentence 21?

A Second,

B Nevertheless,

C Besides,

D Then,

Objective 6

8 The meaning of sentence 22 can be
clarified by changing *it* to —

A the raft

B the bank

C the rapids

D the motor

Objective 6

9 What change, if any, should be made in
sentence 27?

A Change *was over* to **is over**

B Change the comma after *herself* to a
colon

C Change *adventure* to **aventure**

D Make no change

Objective 6

10 What is the most effective way to
improve the organization of the last
paragraph (sentences 24–27)?

A Delete sentence 25

B Move sentence 26 to the end of the
paragraph

C Delete sentence 27

D Move sentence 27 to the beginning
of the paragraph

Objective 6

Name _________________ Class ____________ Date _________ Score ______

Reading: Multiple-Choice Items

1 Ⓐ Ⓑ Ⓒ Ⓓ   5 Ⓐ Ⓑ Ⓒ Ⓓ   9 Ⓐ Ⓑ Ⓒ Ⓓ   13 Ⓐ Ⓑ Ⓒ Ⓓ
2 Ⓐ Ⓑ Ⓒ Ⓓ   6 Ⓐ Ⓑ Ⓒ Ⓓ   10 Ⓐ Ⓑ Ⓒ Ⓓ   14 Ⓐ Ⓑ Ⓒ Ⓓ
3 Ⓐ Ⓑ Ⓒ Ⓓ   7 Ⓐ Ⓑ Ⓒ Ⓓ   11 Ⓐ Ⓑ Ⓒ Ⓓ   15 Ⓐ Ⓑ Ⓒ Ⓓ
4 Ⓐ Ⓑ Ⓒ Ⓓ   8 Ⓐ Ⓑ Ⓒ Ⓓ   12 Ⓐ Ⓑ Ⓒ Ⓓ   16 Ⓐ Ⓑ Ⓒ Ⓓ

Reading: Open-Ended Items

17 ____

____

____

____

18 ____

____

____

____

19 ____

____

____

____

____

____

Writing:
Revising and Editing Passage 1 Items

1 Ⓐ Ⓑ Ⓒ Ⓓ   6 Ⓐ Ⓑ Ⓒ Ⓓ
2 Ⓐ Ⓑ Ⓒ Ⓓ   7 Ⓐ Ⓑ Ⓒ Ⓓ
3 Ⓐ Ⓑ Ⓒ Ⓓ   8 Ⓐ Ⓑ Ⓒ Ⓓ
4 Ⓐ Ⓑ Ⓒ Ⓓ   9 Ⓐ Ⓑ Ⓒ Ⓓ
5 Ⓐ Ⓑ Ⓒ Ⓓ   10 Ⓐ Ⓑ Ⓒ Ⓓ

Revising and Editing Passage 2 Items

1 Ⓐ Ⓑ Ⓒ Ⓓ   6 Ⓐ Ⓑ Ⓒ Ⓓ
2 Ⓐ Ⓑ Ⓒ Ⓓ   7 Ⓐ Ⓑ Ⓒ Ⓓ
3 Ⓐ Ⓑ Ⓒ Ⓓ   8 Ⓐ Ⓑ Ⓒ Ⓓ
4 Ⓐ Ⓑ Ⓒ Ⓓ   9 Ⓐ Ⓑ Ⓒ Ⓓ
5 Ⓐ Ⓑ Ⓒ Ⓓ   10 Ⓐ Ⓑ Ⓒ Ⓓ

Tips for Students: Reading

The Reading section of the TAKS test is designed to see how well you can understand and analyze three different types of pieces dealing with the same theme.

The Reading Triplet

The three components of the TAKS reading triplet are connected by a similar theme or idea. As you move through the three components, you will be required to approach the connecting theme from more than one angle, examining and analyzing the relationships among the three pieces. The three components are:

- A published literary selection
- A published expository, or informational, selection
- A one-page visual representation, such as an advertisement, photograph, or cartoon. Questions for the visual representation will focus on media literacy concepts.

Types of Reading Questions on the TAKS

You will read all three triplet components before beginning to answer questions about them. There will be multiple-choice questions for the individual literary and expository pieces, followed by questions that require you to examine connections between the two selections. Next, you will answer multiple-choice questions about the visual representation. Finally, you will write short-answer responses to open-ended questions about the reading selections, both separately and in comparison to each other.

Strategies for Answering Reading Questions

Use the following suggestions to answer multiple-choice questions on the TAKS reading test:

- First, **read each selection, including the visual representation,** to get a general idea of its topic and tone. Then, ask yourself the following questions about each selection:
  1. What is the topic?
  2. What is the main idea?
  3. What is the purpose of this selection? Is it to inform? to entertain? to persuade?
  4. How does this selection connect to the other two pieces of the triplet?
- Next, **read the questions** on the first selection so you will know what information to look for when you re-read it.
- **Re-read the first selection.** As you read, take notes in the margins or circle information that relates to the questions.
- **Go back to the questions.** Try to answer each one in your own mind before looking at the answer choices.
- Finally, **read all the answer choices** and eliminate those that are obviously incorrect. Then, **choose the best remaining answer**—the one that is closest to the answer you came up with on your own.
- **Repeat** these steps for each set of questions.

To answer the open-ended questions, begin by reading each question twice to understand fully what you are being asked. Think about the question, and go back to the reading selection for information that will help you formulate your answer. As you write your answer, be sure to use specific evidence from the selection to support your response.

TAKS Reading Rubrics

The three short-answer questions appearing on the reading and English Language Arts tests at Grades 9–11 will be scored using the TAKS reading rubrics. Your responses to these three questions will be scored on a four-point scale, with 0 (Insufficient) being the lowest score and 3 (Exemplary) being the highest. Three different reading rubrics will be used to score your responses: the first rubric will score the question attached to the literary selection, the second rubric will score the question attached to the expository selection, and the third rubric will score the question that connects the literary and the expository selections. Your score for each response will be based on your ability to write a reasonable answer and support it with evidence from the selection.

READING RUBRIC—LITERARY SELECTION
OBJECTIVE 2

Score Point 0 — Insufficient
In insufficient responses, the student
- may offer an incorrect theme, character trait, conflict, or change
- may offer a theme, character, conflict, or change that is too general or vague to determine whether it is reasonable
- may incorrectly analyze a literary technique or figurative expression
- may offer an analysis that is too general or vague to determine whether it is reasonable
- may present only a plot summary
- may not address the question in any way or may answer a different question than the one asked
- may offer only incomplete or irrelevant textual evidence

In addition, insufficient responses may lack clarity.

Score Point 1 — Partially Sufficient
In partially sufficient responses, the student
- may offer a reasonable theme, character trait, conflict, or change but provide only general, incomplete, or partially accurate/relevant textual evidence or provide no textual evidence at all
- may offer a reasonable analysis of a literary technique or figurative expression but provide only general, incomplete, or partially accurate/relevant textual evidence or provide no textual evidence at all
- may offer a reasonable idea or analysis and may provide textual evidence, but this evidence is only weakly connected to the idea or analysis
- may offer accurate/relevant textual evidence without providing an idea or analysis

In addition, partially sufficient responses may be somewhat unclear or vague.

Score Point 2 — Sufficient
In sufficient responses, the student
- must offer a reasonable theme, character trait, conflict, or change and support it with accurate/relevant textual evidence
- must offer a reasonable analysis of a literary technique or figurative expression and support it with accurate/relevant textual evidence

In addition, sufficient responses must be clear and specific.

Score Point 3 — Exemplary

In exemplary responses, the student

- must offer a particularly thoughtful or insightful theme, character trait, conflict, or change and strongly support it with accurate/relevant textual evidence
- must offer a particularly thoughtful or insightful analysis of a literary technique or figurative expression and strongly support it with accurate/relevant textual evidence

In addition, exemplary responses must demonstrate the student's depth of understanding and ability to effectively connect textual evidence to the idea or analysis.

Evidence may consist of a direct quotation, a paraphrase, or a specific synopsis.

READING RUBRIC—EXPOSITORY SELECTION
OBJECTIVE 3

Score Point 0 — Insufficient

In insufficient responses, the student

- may draw a conclusion, offer an interpretation, or make a prediction that is not based on the text
- may draw a conclusion, offer an interpretation, or make a prediction that does not address the question
- may draw a conclusion, offer an interpretation, or make a prediction that is not reasonable
- may draw a conclusion, offer an interpretation, or make a prediction that is too general or vague to determine whether it is reasonable
- may incorrectly analyze or evaluate a characteristic of the text
- may not address the question in any way or may answer a different question than the one asked
- may offer only incomplete or irrelevant textual evidence

In addition, insufficient responses may lack clarity.

Score Point 1 — Partially Sufficient

In partially sufficient responses, the student

- may draw a reasonable conclusion, offer a reasonable interpretation, or make a reasonable prediction that is supported only by general, incomplete, or partially accurate/relevant textual evidence or provide no textual evidence at all
- may offer a reasonable analysis or evaluation of a characteristic of the text that is supported only by general, incomplete, or partially accurate/relevant textual evidence or provide no textual evidence at all
- may offer a reasonable idea, analysis, or evaluation and may provide textual evidence, but this evidence is only weakly connected to the idea, analysis, or evaluation
- may offer accurate/relevant textual evidence without drawing a conclusion, offering an interpretation, making a prediction, or providing an analysis or evaluation

In addition, partially sufficient responses may be somewhat unclear or vague.

Score Point 2 — Sufficient

In sufficient responses, the student

- must draw a reasonable conclusion, offer a reasonable interpretation, or make a reasonable prediction and must support it with accurate/relevant textual evidence
- must offer a reasonable analysis or evaluation of a characteristic of the selection and must support it with accurate/relevant textual evidence

In addition, sufficient responses must be clear and specific.

Score Point 3 — Exemplary

In exemplary responses, the student

- must offer a particularly thoughtful or insightful conclusion, interpretation, or prediction and strongly support it with accurate/relevant textual evidence
- must offer a particularly thoughtful or insightful analysis or evaluation of a characteristic of the text and strongly support it with accurate/relevant textual evidence

In addition, exemplary responses show strong evidence of the student's depth of understanding and ability to effectively connect textual evidence to the idea, analysis, or evaluation.

Evidence may consist of a direct quotation, a paraphrase, or a specific synopsis.

READING RUBRIC—LITERARY/EXPOSITORY CROSSOVER
OBJECTIVE 3

Score Point 0 — Insufficient

In insufficient responses, the student

- may draw a conclusion, offer an interpretation, or make a prediction that is not based on the selections
- may draw a conclusion, offer an interpretation, or make a prediction that does not address the question
- may draw a conclusion, offer an interpretation, or make a prediction that is not reasonable
- may draw a conclusion, offer an interpretation, or make a prediction that is too general or vague to determine whether it is reasonable
- may incorrectly analyze or evaluate a characteristic of text based on both selections
- may not address the question in any way or may answer a different question than the one asked
- may offer only incomplete or irrelevant textual evidence from one or both selections

In addition, insufficient responses may lack clarity.

Score Point 1 — Partially Sufficient

In partially sufficient responses, the student

- may draw a reasonable conclusion, offer a reasonable interpretation, or make a reasonable prediction that is based on both selections but supported only by general, incomplete, or partially accurate/relevant textual evidence from one or both selections
- may draw a reasonable conclusion, offer a reasonable interpretation, or make a reasonable prediction but may offer textual support from only one selection or may offer no textual support at all
- may offer a reasonable analysis or evaluation of a characteristic of text based on both selections that is supported only by general, incomplete, or partially accurate/relevant textual evidence from one or both selections
- may offer a reasonable analysis or evaluation of a characteristic of text based on both selections but may offer textual support from only one selection or may offer no textual support at all
- may offer a reasonable idea, analysis, or evaluation based on both selections and may provide textual evidence from both selections, but this evidence is only weakly connected to the idea, analysis, or evaluation
- may offer accurate/relevant textual evidence from both selections but may draw a conclusion, offer an interpretation, make a prediction, or provide an analysis or evaluation based on only one selection
- may offer accurate/relevant textual evidence from both selections without drawing a conclusion, offering an interpretation, making a prediction, or providing an analysis or evaluation

In addition, partially sufficient responses may be somewhat unclear or vague or may indicate that the student has difficulty making connections across selections.

Score Point 2 — Sufficient

In sufficient responses, the student

- must draw a reasonable conclusion, offer a reasonable interpretation, or make a reasonable prediction based on both selections and must support it with accurate/relevant textual evidence from both selections
- must offer a reasonable analysis or evaluation of a characteristic of text based on both selections and must support it with accurate/relevant textual evidence from both selections

In addition, sufficient responses indicate that the student is able to make clear and specific connections across selections.

Score Point 3 — Exemplary

In exemplary responses, the student

- must offer a particularly thoughtful or insightful conclusion, interpretation, or prediction based on both selections and strongly support it with accurate/relevant textual evidence from both selections
- must offer a particularly thoughtful or insightful analysis or evaluation of a characteristic of text based on both selections and strongly support it with accurate/relevant textual evidence from both selections

In addition, exemplary responses indicate that the student is able to make meaningful connections across selections. These responses show strong evidence of the student's depth of understanding and ability to effectively connect textual evidence to the idea, analysis, or evaluation.

Evidence may consist of a direct quotation, a paraphrase, or a specific synopsis.

Tips for Students: Writing

The Writing portion of the TAKS test consists of a writing prompt and one or more Revising and Editing passages with accompanying multiple-choice questions.

Strategies for Responding to the Writing Prompt
- First, **read the writing prompt carefully** and make sure you understand what it is asking you to do. Think about the prompt, and jot down some ideas. What comes to mind as you think about the topic?
- Next, **think about what you will write.** The TAKS test allows you to respond to the writing prompt with any type of prose composition that you choose; in other words, you are free to write a short story, a journal entry, a magazine article, an essay, a letter to the editor, or any other type of writing, except poetry. However, remember that more important are the organization and ideas in your response, not the form you choose.
- **Organize your thoughts** by sketching out a plan for what you want to say. Begin by determining the main idea that you would like to communicate with your writing, and then plan how you will develop that idea—for example, with description, examples, or anecdotes. The better your plan, the easier it will be to develop your composition effectively.
- **Create your first draft,** following the plan you developed.
- **Edit and proofread** your first draft by completing the following steps:
  1. Check that you have responded to the writing prompt and that your theme or main idea is clear. Add, delete, or rearrange sentences as needed to make your theme or main idea come through effectively.
  2. Check that the tone of your writing is suitable for the type of composition you have chosen and that your language is precise and vivid.
  3. Check to see that your voice—your own unique way of expressing yourself—comes through in your writing. In other words, does your composition sound as if anyone could have written it, or does it sound as if it could have come only from you?
  4. Check for spelling and punctuation errors, run-on sentences, and sentence fragments. Make sure you have used verb tenses correctly.
- Finally, **create a final draft** of your paper, incorporating all of the revisions and corrections you have made.

Strategies for Answering the Revising and Editing Multiple-Choice Questions
The Revising and Editing passages consist of a short essay such as one of your peers might write for a science, history, or other class. You are asked to proofread the essay and answer multiple-choice questions about its organization, spelling, grammar, and punctuation. Here are some suggestions for answering the questions.
- **Read the passage** once to get a feel for its content and structure. Circle anything that strikes you as incorrect on this first reading; you may find a question about it later.
- **Try to answer each question** before looking at the answer choices. For example, if a question says, "What change, if any, should be made in sentence 6?" re-read sentence 6 to see if you can identify a spelling, grammar, or punctuation error in it.
- **Choose the answer choice** that matches the error you identified, or if you didn't identify an error, examine each answer choice and determine which one relates to an error in the passage.

TAKS Writing Rubric

Your response to the writing prompt will be scored on a four-point scale, with 1 being the lowest score and 4 being the highest. The rubric, or grading scale, is based on five categories: focus and coherence, organization, development of ideas, voice, and conventions. These categories will be given equal weight when each response is scored. The same writing rubric will be used to score compositions for all grades in which the TAKS test is given.

SCORE POINT 1

EACH COMPOSITION AT THIS SCORE POINT IS AN INEFFECTIVE PRESENTATION OF THE WRITER'S IDEAS.

Focus and Coherence
- Individual paragraphs and/or the composition as a whole are not focused. The writer may shift abruptly from idea to idea, making it difficult for the reader to understand how the ideas included in the composition are related.
- The composition as a whole has little, or no, sense of completeness. The introduction and conclusion, if present, may be perfunctory.
- A substantial amount of writing may be extraneous because it does not contribute to the development or quality of the composition. In some cases, the composition overall may be only weakly connected to the prompt.

Organization
- The writer's progression of thought from sentence to sentence and/or paragraph to paragraph is not logical. Sometimes weak progression results from an absence of transitions or from the use of transitions that do not make sense. At other times, the progression of thought is simply not evident, even if appropriate transitions are included.
- An organizational strategy is not evident. The writer may present ideas in a random or haphazard way, making the composition difficult to follow.
- Wordiness and/or repetition may stall the progression of ideas.

Development of Ideas
- The writer presents one or more ideas but provides little or no development of those ideas.
- The writer presents one or more ideas and attempts to develop them. However, this development is so general or vague that it prevents the reader from understanding the writer's ideas.
- The writer presents only a plot summary of a published piece of writing, a movie, or a television show.
- The writer omits information, which creates significant gaps between ideas. These gaps prevent the reader from clearly understanding those ideas.

Voice
- The writer does not engage the reader, therefore failing to establish a connection.
- There may be little or no sense of the writer's individual voice. The composition does not sound authentic or original. The writer is unable to express his/her individuality or unique perspective.

Conventions
- There is little or no evidence in the composition that the writer can correctly apply the conventions of the English language. Severe and/or frequent errors in spelling, capitalization, punctuation, grammar, usage, and sentence structure may cause the writing to be unclear or difficult to read. These errors weaken the composition by causing an overall lack of fluency.
- The writer may misuse or omit words and phrases and may frequently write awkward sentences. These weaknesses interfere with the effective communication of ideas.

SCORE POINT 2

EACH COMPOSITION AT THIS SCORE POINT IS A SOMEWHAT EFFECTIVE PRESENTATION OF THE WRITER'S IDEAS.

Focus and Coherence
- Individual paragraphs and/or the composition as a whole are somewhat focused. The writer may shift quickly from idea to idea, but the reader has no difficulty understanding how the ideas included in the composition are related.
- The composition as a whole has some sense of completeness. The writer includes an introduction and conclusion, but they may be superficial.
- Some of the writing may be extraneous because it does not contribute to the development or quality of the composition as a whole.

Organization
- The writer's progression of thought from sentence to sentence and/or paragraph to paragraph may not always be smooth or completely logical. Sometimes the writer needs to strengthen the progression by including more meaningful transitions; at other times the writer simply needs to establish a clearer link between ideas.
- The organizational strategy or strategies the writer chooses do not enable the writer to present ideas effectively.
- Some wordiness and/or repetition may be evident, but these weaknesses do not completely stall the progression of ideas.

Development of Ideas
- The writer attempts to develop the composition by listing ideas or briefly explaining them. In both of these cases, the development remains superficial, limiting the reader's understanding and appreciation of the writer's ideas.
- The writer presents one or more ideas and attempts to develop them. However, there is little evidence of depth of thinking because this development may be somewhat general, inconsistent, or contrived.
- The writer may omit small pieces of information that create minor gaps between ideas. However, these gaps do not prevent the reader from understanding those ideas.

Voice
- There may be moments when the writer engages the reader but fails to sustain the connection.
- Individual paragraphs or sections of the composition may sound authentic or original, but the writer has difficulty expressing his/her individuality or unique perspective.

Conventions
- Errors in spelling, capitalization, punctuation, grammar, usage, and sentence structure throughout the composition may indicate a limited control of conventions. Although these errors do not cause the writing to be unclear, they weaken the overall fluency of the composition.
- The writer may include some simple or inaccurate words and phrases and may write some awkward sentences. These weaknesses limit the overall effectiveness of the communication of ideas.

SCORE POINT 3

EACH COMPOSITION AT THIS SCORE POINT IS A GENERALLY EFFECTIVE
PRESENTATION OF THE WRITER'S IDEAS.

Focus and Coherence

- Individual paragraphs and the composition as a whole are, for the most part, focused. The writer generally shows the clear relationship between ideas, making few sudden shifts from one idea to the next.
- The composition as a whole has a sense of completeness. The introduction and conclusion add some depth to the composition.
- Most of the writing contributes to the development or quality of the composition as a whole.

Organization

- The writer's progression of thought from sentence to sentence and paragraph to paragraph is generally smooth and controlled. For the most part, transitions are meaningful, and the links between ideas are logical.
- The organizational strategy or strategies the writer chooses are generally effective.
- Wordiness and/or repetition, if present, are minor problems that do not stall the progression of ideas.

Development of Ideas

- The writer attempts to develop all the ideas included in the composition. Although some ideas may be developed more thoroughly and specifically than others, the development overall reflects some depth of thought, enabling the reader to generally understand and appreciate the writer's ideas.
- The writer's presentation of some ideas may be thoughtful. There may be little evidence that the writer has been willing to take compositional risks when developing the topic.

Voice

- The writer engages the reader and sustains that connection throughout most of the composition.
- For the most part, the composition sounds authentic and original. The writer is generally able to express his/her individuality or unique perspective.

Conventions

- The writer generally demonstrates a good command of spelling, capitalization, punctuation, grammar, usage, and sentence structure. Although the writer may make minor errors, they create few disruptions in the fluency of the composition.
- The words, phrases, and sentence structures the writer uses are generally appropriate and contribute to the overall effectiveness of the communication of ideas.

<h1 style="text-align:center">SCORE POINT 4</h1>

EACH COMPOSITION AT THIS SCORE POINT IS A HIGHLY EFFECTIVE
PRESENTATION OF THE WRITER'S IDEAS.

Focus and Coherence

- Individual paragraphs and the composition as a whole are focused. This sustained focus enables the reader to understand and appreciate how the ideas included in the composition are related.
- The composition as a whole has a sense of completeness. The introduction and conclusion are meaningful because they add depth to the composition.
- Most, if not all, of the writing contributes to the development or quality of the composition as a whole.

Organization

- The writer's progression of thought from sentence to sentence and paragraph to paragraph is smooth and controlled. The writer's use of meaningful transitions and the logical movement from idea to idea strengthen this progression.
- The organizational strategy or strategies the writer chooses enhance the writer's ability to present ideas clearly and effectively.

Development of Ideas

- The writer's thorough and specific development of each idea creates depth of thought in the composition, enabling the reader to truly understand and appreciate the writer's ideas.
- The writer's presentation of ideas is thoughtful or insightful. The writer may approach the topic from an unusual perspective, use his/her unique experiences or view of the world as a basis for writing, or make interesting connections between ideas. In all these cases, the writer's willingness to take compositional risks enhances the quality of the content.

Voice

- The writer engages the reader and sustains this connection throughout the composition.
- The composition sounds authentic and original. The writer is able to express his/her individuality or unique perspective.

Conventions

- The overall strength of the conventions contributes to the effectiveness of the composition. The writer demonstrates a consistent command of spelling, capitalization, punctuation, grammar, usage, and sentence structure. When the writer attempts to communicate complex ideas through sophisticated forms of expression, he/she may make minor errors as a result of these compositional risks. These types of errors do not detract from the overall fluency of the composition.
- The words, phrases, and sentence structures the writer uses enhance the overall effectiveness of the communication of ideas.